I Love Planes

By Lisa Regan
Illustrated by Terry Pastor

Miles Kelly

First published in 2009 by Miles Kelly Publishing Ltd
Bardfield Centre, Great Bardfield, Essex, CM7 4SL

2 4 6 8 10 9 7 5 3 1

Editorial Director Belinda Gallagher
Art Director Jo Brewer
Editorial Assistant Toby Tippen
Designer Joe Jones
Cover Artworker Carmen Johnson
Production Manager Elizabeth Brunwin
Reprographics Stephan Davis, Ian Paulyn
Archive Manager Jennifer Hunt

ISBN 978-1-84810-036-7

Printed in Thailand

ACKNOWLEDGEMENTS
Page 4 Monica Minford/Fotolia.com; 13 Jonathan
Brizendine/Fotolia.com; 14 Matthew Boggs/Fotolia.com;
18 Ronen/Fotolia.com; 21 Tomasz Pawlowski/Fotolia.com;
23 Tomasz Pawlowski/Fotolia.com

All other images from the Miles Kelly Archives

British Library Cataloguing-in-Publication Data
A catalogue record for this book is available
from the British Library

Made with paper from a sustainable forest
www.mileskelly.net   info@mileskelly.net

www.factsforprojects.com

Contents

Firefighting plane

Some planes can help to put out fires. Sometimes, a fire breaks out in an area that fire engines cannot reach, such as in a forest. Special planes can scoop up water then dump it over a fire. This helps to stop the fire from spreading and causing too much damage.

Hover power

Helicopters can also fight fires. They carry buckets of water, which they dump over the flames.

Tanks inside the plane are filled with water. To fill them, the plane flies over a lake or the sea and scoops the water up.

floats on the wings allow the plane to take off or land on water.

The tanks are opened to let the water gush out and put out the fire.

Passenger airliner

Every day, passenger airliners carry millions of people all over the world. The biggest airliner is the Airbus A380. It can carry more than 800 people. At the airport, the plane is loaded with luggage before the passengers board.

The plane has a double deck, which means that passengers can sit upstairs or downstairs.

Sitting down

The main area inside an airliner is the cabin. This is where the passengers sit during their flight.

During take-off, engines speed the plane along the runway. In the sky, they power the plane through the air.

6

When it is flying, the Airbus A380 travels at 900 kilometres an hour.

AEROLINES

SUPERAIR

A380 AIRBUS

Inside the front part of the plane is the cockpit. This is where the pilots sit to fly the plane.

Fighter jet

A fighter jet is a small plane used by armed forces during wars. This jet is an F-22 Raptor, and it is used to search for and attack enemy planes. It is loaded with bombs and weapons, and has a machine gun in one of its wings. It is difficult for the enemy to track down this jet because it is very fast.

The F-22 Raptor is thought to be the best fighter jet in the world.

Only one pilot can fit into the tiny cockpit of this plane.

Jump jet

Instead of speeding along a runway, a jump jet takes off straight up into the air. A jet of gas from the plane's engines shoots downwards, and pushes the plane up. The jet can also hover in the air.

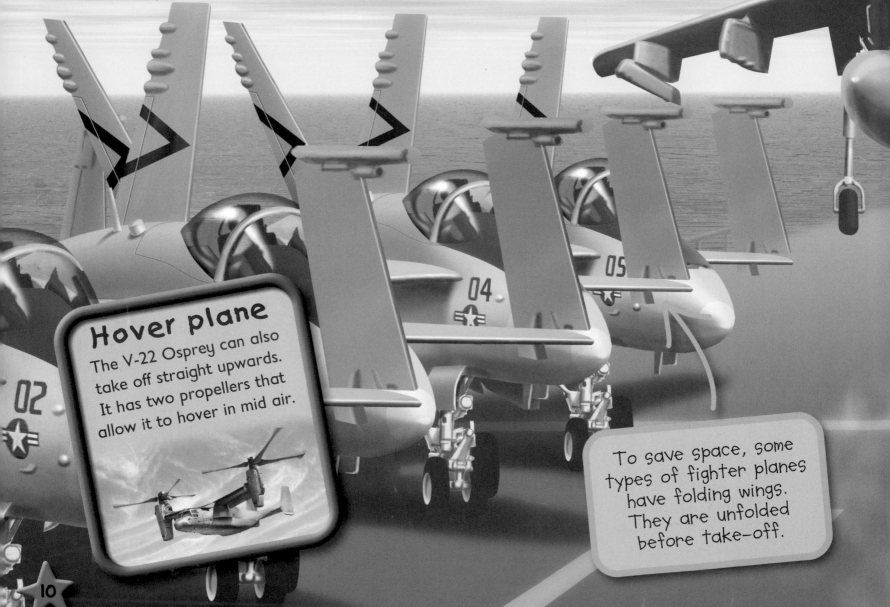

Hover plane
The V-22 Osprey can also take off straight upwards. It has two propellers that allow it to hover in mid air.

To save space, some types of fighter planes have folding wings. They are unfolded before take-off.

This jet is called a Harrier. The pilot is guided into the air by a crewman. He signals that it is safe for the jet to take off.

For take-off, nozzles on the engines swing to face downwards. Hot gases push the plane up until it is hovering like a helicopter.

Jump jets usually take off from giant ships called aircraft carriers.

Transport plane

The Antonov AN-225 is the biggest, heaviest plane in the world. It has six engines to provide the power the plane needs to take off and fly in the air. This huge aircraft is powerful enough to transport a space shuttle. Only two have ever been built.

The inside of the plane is designed to carry big items. It has room to hold about 80 cars!

The unusual tail shape helps the plane stay in the air even when it is carrying heavy loads.

There are 14 wheels on each side, underneath the plane. They are used for landing and take-off.

This space shuttle has been fixed to the back of the plane. It is being flown to its launch site.

Cargo plane

This huge Galaxy plane also carries heavy items. The nose opens up to allow big items to be loaded.

Stealth bomber

The stealth bomber is difficult to spot. A special coating on its bodywork makes the plane harder to track on a radar screen. Two stealth planes carrying bombs can do the same job as 75 ordinary fighter planes. Stealth planes are also used for spying on secret sites.

The smooth, curved shape helps the plane fly at high speeds.

This plane is called the B-2 Spirit. Only 21 B-2s have ever been made.

The B-2 can travel 10,000 kilometres without having to stop for fuel.

14

Odd shape

The shape of the B-2 makes it look like a big, flying wing. This also makes it difficult to spot.

Four jet engines give the plane enough power to fly at 760 kilometres an hour.

The plane only has room for two pilots. It also has a flushing toilet!

Seaplane

This plane can take off and land on water. It also has wheels, so it can use a runway like other planes. Seaplanes are used for rescue and pleasure trips, as well as by people who live on small islands.

The wings are placed high up, on top of the plane. This stops it wobbling when it is flying.

Two floats beneath the plane's body keep it out of the water.

Flying boat

A flying boat is a plane that takes off and lands on water. It doesn't have floats and the body of the plane rests on the water.

Small planes often have a propeller instead of jet engines.

Business jet

This small jet is often used to fly people to important meetings. People can travel without waiting at an airport for a bigger passenger plane. Inside the cabin are comfortable seats with cushions, tables and carpets.

It costs around £10 million to buy a business jet.

Winglets at the end of the wings help the plane fly more efficiently so it uses less fuel.

Airshow

There are many different types of planes at an airshow. Some are parked on the ground for visitors to take a closer look at. There are also displays in the sky to see how fast the planes can go, or to watch them perform stunts.

This World War II bomber is called a Flying Fortress. It could carry ten crew, plus bombs and guns.

A plane with two parts to each wing is called a bi-plane. This bi-plane was used to train British pilots for World War II.

This fighter pilot shows off his skills, performing somersaults in the air for people watching below.

"Fuddy Duddy"

The Flying Fortress has a big window. This is where the crew sat to look out for and fire at enemies.

Hangar
Planes are kept in hangars until they are needed for an airshow. A hangar is like a huge car garage!

Red Arrows

The Royal Air Force has a stunt team that performs amazing displays. The team is called the Red Arrows because the planes are bright red. There are nine planes that can release coloured trails in the sky to make their stunts look even more fantastic.

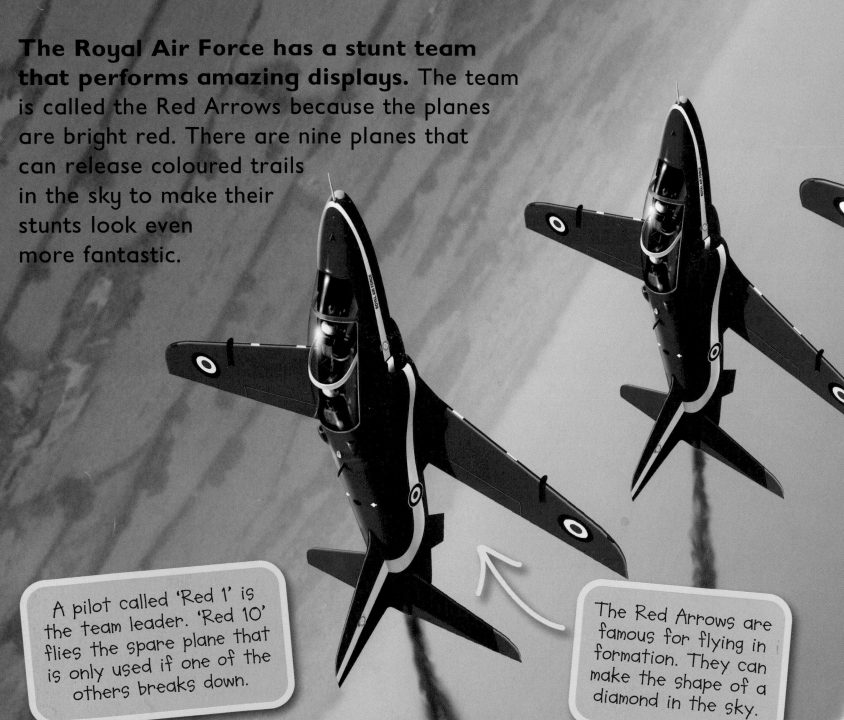

A pilot called 'Red 1' is the team leader. 'Red 10' flies the spare plane that is only used if one of the others breaks down.

The Red Arrows are famous for flying in formation. They can make the shape of a diamond in the sky.

The planes are not real fighter jets, but trainer planes that cost less money.

Blue Angels
The United States navy uses a team of Blue Angels to perform shows like the Red Arrows.

Three new pilots join the Red Arrows team each year. The other pilots help them to learn very quickly.

Fun facts

Firefighting plane As well as water, firefighting planes may dump a special red powder over a fire to try to put out the flames.

Passenger airliner Under the floor of the main cabin is an area called the hold. This is where most of the passengers' luggage is stored.

Raptor fighter jet The F-22 can fly at over 2000 kilometres an hour!

Jump jet The Harrier jump jet is known as a VTOL plane. This stands for Vertical Take-Off and Landing.

Transport plane The AN-225 weighs 600 tonnes. It can carry a load of up to 200 tonnes.

Stealth bomber To stop the special coating on the B-2's bodywork from being destroyed, the plane is kept in an air-conditioned hangar when not in use.

Seaplane Any luggage can be stored inside the plane's floats!

Business jet There are around 11,000 business jets worldwide.

Airshow The Royal International Air Tattoo is the world's largest military airshow. It lasts for two days and up to 200,000 people visit on both days.

Red Arrows The flying team was formed in 1965 and has flown more than 4000 displays in over 50 countries.